Your

Travel

Guide to

ANCIENT
ISRAEL

Your

Travel

Guide to

ANCIENT
ISRAEL

Josepha Sherman

LERNER PUBLICATIONS COMPANY • MINNEAPOLIS

Note to reader regarding B.C.E. and C.E.: Israel's history spans both ancient and modern times. Some books use the abbreviations B.C. ("before
Christ") and A.D. (*anno Domini*, or "in the year of our Lord") to date ancient and modern events. This dating system is based on the birth of Jesus, orginally thought to have occurred in A.D. 1. This book uses an
alternative method that does not refer to Jesus. We use the abbreviations
B.C.E., or "before the common era," instead of B.C. We use C.E., or "of the
common era," instead of A.D.

Copyright © 2004 by Josepha Sherman

Lerner Publications Company
A division of Lerner Publishing Group
241 First Avenue North
Minneapolis, MN 55401 U.S.A.

Website address: www.lernerbooks.com

Library of Congress Cataloging-in-Publication Data

Sherman, Josepha.
    Your travel guide to ancient Israel / by Josepha Sherman.
       p.   cm. — (Passport to history)
    Includes bibliographical references and index.
    Summary: Takes readers on a journey back in time in order to experience life in
Israel at the time of King Solomon, describing clothing, accommodations, foods,
local customs, transportation, a few notable personalities, and more.
    ISBN: 0–8225–3072–4 (lib. bdg. : alk. paper)
    1. Palestine—Description and travel—Juvenile literature. 2. Israel—Description
and travel—Juvenile literature. [1. Palestine—Description and travel. 2. Israel—
Description and travel. 3. Palestine—Social life and customs—To A.D. 70] I. Title.
II. Passport to history (Minneapolis, MN.)
DS104.S54   2004
933'.02—dc21   2003005622

Manufactured in the United States of America
1 2 3 4 5 6 – JR – 09 08 07 06 05 04

CONTENTS

INTRODUCTION

GETTING STARTED

Welcome to Passport to History. You will be traveling through time and space to ancient Israel in the eighth century B.C.E. This travel guide will answer questions such as:

- ➤ **What's going on in ancient Israel?**
- ➤ **Which local foods should I try?**
- ➤ **Who will I meet while I'm there?**
- ➤ **Where should I stay?**
- ➤ **What do I wear?**

Remember that you are going back in time to a distant culture. Some of the things that you own didn't exist during this period. They didn't have cameras. (That's why the pictures in this book are either drawings or photographs made after the invention of photography.) They didn't have electricity either. So forget about packing your video games, hair dryers, watches, cell phones, and the other modern conveniences that would make your stay in ancient Israel a bit more comfortable. But if you read this guide, you'll be able to do as the locals do—and they manage just fine, as you will see.

The mountains of ancient Israel still rise above the deserts in modern Israel.

NOTE TO THE TRAVELER

The ancient Israelites left literature, official documents, artwork, tools, and the remains of buildings that provide a window into their lives. In addition, they gave us three of the world's major religions, Judaism, Christianity, and Islam. Archaeologists study the remains of ancient Israelite structures and examine the remains of artifacts that have survived. Historians study texts left by ancient writers, such as Flavius Josephus, who lived from about 37 to 100 C.E. He wrote *Antiquities of the Jews,* a history from the biblical creation to 66 C.E. Historians also study religious writings, such as the Tanach (the Jewish Holy Scriptures), and the Christian Bible.

WHY VISIT ANCIENT ISRAEL?

It is 800 B.C.E., and ancient Israel hasn't been a united country for very long. In fact, it has only had three kings in its history so far: Saul, David, and the current ruler, King David's son, King Solomon. Before that, the area was divided into lands ruled by peoples such as the Canaanites and the Philistines. In the short time that ancient Israel has been a united kingdom, it has become a land of major importance. Read on to see why.

Check out the map. You'll see that ancient Israel isn't really very large. But it has trading ties with all the major empires around the Mediterranean Sea and in Asia. These include Egypt, Phoenicia (modern-day Lebanon), India, and even Spain in Europe. Egypt, one of the world's mightiest kingdoms, has promised peace with ancient Israel.

Under King Solomon's rule, ancient Israel has also become known as a major center for learning and the arts. Rulers of countries as far away as Sheba (also known as Saba, probably present-day Yemen) sometimes send representatives to test the king's wisdom and the learning of his people. It's possible that Sheba's queen made the long journey to visit Solomon herself.

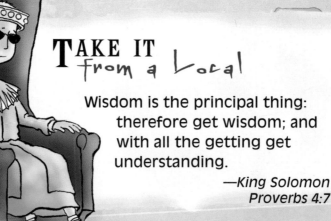

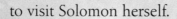
TAKE IT from a Local

Wisdom is the principal thing: therefore get wisdom; and with all the getting get understanding.

—*King Solomon*
Proverbs 4:7

EGYPT

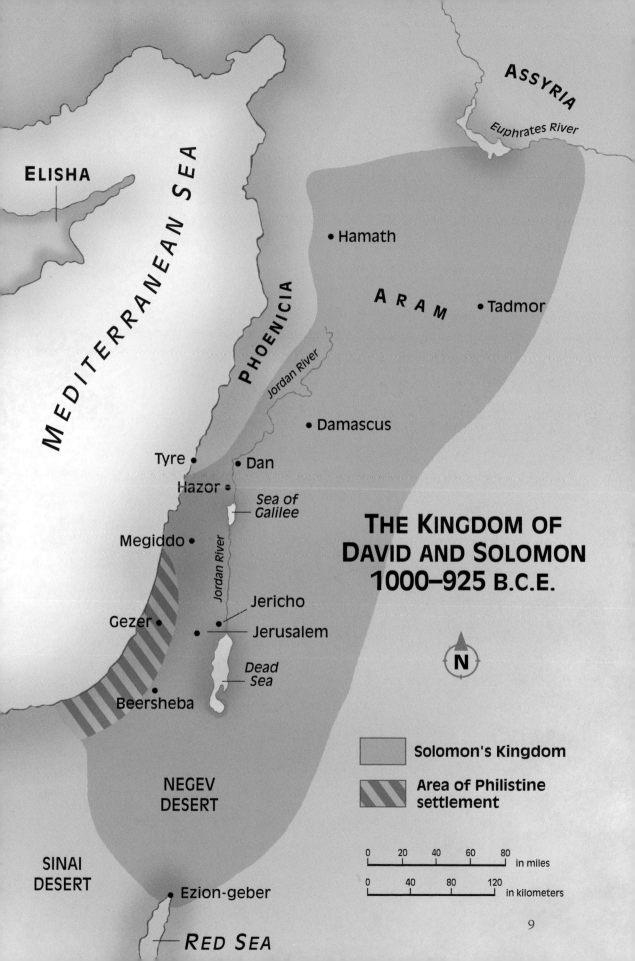

ASSYRIA

Euphrates River

ELISHA

MEDITERRANEAN SEA

PHOENICIA

A R A M

• Hamath

• Tadmor

Jordan River

• Damascus

Tyre •

• Dan

Hazor •

Sea of Galilee

Megiddo •

Jordan River

THE KINGDOM OF
DAVID AND SOLOMON
1000–925 B.C.E.

Jericho

Gezer •

• Jerusalem

Dead Sea

N

Beersheba •

NEGEV
DESERT

Solomon's Kingdom

Area of Philistine
settlement

SINAI
DESERT

| 0 | 20 | 40 | 60 | 80 | |
in miles

| 0 | 40 | 80 | 120 | |
in kilometers

• Ezion-geber

RED SEA

9

THE BASICS

LOCATION LOWDOWN

Ancient Israel includes several different types of landscape and has some really spectacular scenery. In the south and southwest lies the Negev Desert, which is a barren, wild yet beautiful place. It's full of canyons and wadis (dry streambeds) and sheer cliffs of red sandstone. You won't want to go here without a guide though, since water is difficult to find. The desert heat can kill the unwary. A finger of the Red Sea reaches into the southern part of the Negev.

To the west, ancient Israel borders the Mediterranean Sea. Here you'll find long stretches of lovely beaches and the chance to get in some good swimming. Remember, though, that bathing suits haven't been invented yet, and people in the area don't approve of public nudity! It may not be safe to swim in a totally isolated place, either, because there may be dangerous currents. Be aware that clothing left on the beach while you swim might be stolen. But even if you don't go swimming, you can enjoy gorgeous views of sparkling blue waves hitting the shore.

To the north, much of the land is rocky and rugged, beautiful but potentially dangerous. In the northeast are the steep, dark cliffs known in modern times as the Golan Heights. These are made of the volcanic rock called basalt and were formed long ago by volcanic eruptions. You don't have to worry about that happening again. Volcanoes are no longer active in the land. The steep cliffs make it a good place for fortresses, though, and possible ambushes by bandits, but not a good place for careless tourists.

Mountains run down the length of Israel. The famous hills of Galilee rise to about four thousand feet above sea level. There are many rolling hills and rocky hilltops, some of which are dotted with the silver green of olive trees.

The hot, dry Negev Desert can be brutal—or even fatal—to the inexperienced traveler. Be sure to hire a guide before setting out!

In ancient and modern times, the Dead Sea has been known to crust over with salt.

The Jordan River flows through the center of ancient Israel. In the north, the river widens into the Sea of Galilee. In the south, it runs into the Dead Sea, the lowest point on the earth's surface. The Dead Sea is so salty that almost nothing can live in it.

Most of the Jordan River is great for fishing, although in ancient Israel fishing is usually done with nets, not with a fishing rod. But even if you aren't interested in fishing, you're sure to be impressed by the power of the wide river itself and enjoy the lovely green landscape around it.

CLIMATE

Ancient Israel is mostly a desert land. In many areas, it's too hot for even the most fanatically foolish sunbathers. You can easily find several different types of weather, though, depending on what season it is.

In the summer, ancient Israel can be dangerously hot, especially in the south. That nice long coastline on the Mediterranean will provide some relief from the heat because cool breezes blow in steadily off the water. Some of the mountains are tall enough to be dusted with snow in the winter, and sometimes you can catch a cool breeze blowing down from one of them.

In the late fall into the winter is the rainy season, which is the main time for crops to grow. In ancient Israel, the first rains tend to fall in what we call October, but the true rainy season comes between December and February. More rain falls in the northwestern section of ancient Israel and less to the southeast.

It almost never grows cold enough to snow in the winter, other than that occasional dusting on the higher peaks. But the rainy season can turn really chilly, and the dampness gets into everything. You're best off timing your visit for spring or early autumn, when the weather is neither too hot nor too damp and chilly.

The clothing you bring will depend not only on the local fashions but also on the type of weather you expect to encounter. Unless you plan to visit ancient Israel in the chilly, damp winter, you'll want to look into clothing that will keep you cool but still protect you from the desert sun. Take some type of sun hat. Remember that you can't buy sunscreen in ancient Israel!

Of course, no matter what climate you expect to find, you won't want to stand out too much by wearing something too modern such as sneakers or a name-brand jacket. Remember that the people of ancient Israel have different standards of what's proper. Leave your cutoffs or shorts at home. Such revealing clothing would be considered shocking, if not downright rude.

Local Time

Remember when planning your trip that the ancient Israelites don't use the same calendar that we use in the modern United States. Unless you work things out in advance, you might find yourself visiting someone on the wrong day or even in the wrong month.

The calendar we use in modern times is called the Gregorian calendar after Pope Gregory XIII, who made it the official European calendar back in 1582. The length of its months is based on the time that the earth takes to revolve around the sun. The calendar that is used in ancient Israel has twelve months, just like the modern American calendar—but it's a lunar calendar, which is based not on the sun but on the cycles of the moon. Each month in ancient Israel begins on the night of the new moon and lasts until the next new moon.

If you do a little math, you'll see that the twelve-month count in ancient Israel doesn't quite equal a year. The lunar calendar adds up to 354 days, not to our modern calendar's 365 days. This means that there are eleven days left over! So what do the local people do with those extra eleven days? About every three years, they add one month of twenty-nine days in the winter. This is ancient Israel's version of a leap year. In modern times, by the way, the Israeli lunar calendar is still used in Israel, by observant Jews around the world, and in many parts of the Arab world.

Here is a comparison, month by month, of one version of an ancient Israeli lunar calendar and the modern American calendar.

ISRAELITE MONTH	MODERN AMERICAN MONTH
1. Nissan, 30 days	March–April
2. Iyar, 29 days	April–May
3. Sivan, 30 days	May–June
4. Tammuz, 29 days	June–July
5. Ab, 30 days	July–August
6. Elul, 29 days	August–September
7. Tishri, 30 days	September–October
8. Heshvan, 29 or 30 days	October–November
9. Kislev, 29 or 30 days	November–December
10. Tebet, 29 days	December–January
11. Shebat, 30 days	January–February
12. Adar, 29 or 30 days	February–March
13. Adar II 29 days	added winter month

Unlike the widely used Gregorian calendar, which is based on the cycles of the sun, the Jewish calendar follows the phases of the moon. This portion of a Jewish calendar was made in the 1800s.

A scribe copies the words from a scroll onto a fresh roll of parchment. This document is in Hebrew, one of the many languages heard on the streets of ancient Israel's cities.

LANGUAGE LESSON

The language you're most likely to hear in ancient Israel is Hebrew, the language of the Israelites themselves. In fact, the Israelites are also called Hebrews.

You probably already know that Hebrew is still spoken in the modern world. However, modern Hebrew has added a lot of words, including words for computers and televisions.

But in the streets of ancient Israel's cities, you're also very likely to hear another language. This is Aramaic, which is closely related to Hebrew. Aramaic has become the language used by merchants from all

Back TO THE FUTURE

So popular was Aramaic that, after the time of Solomon, it gradually took the place of Hebrew. In the early years of the Christian era, Jesus, the founder of Christianity, and some of his followers spoke Aramaic in ancient Israel.

over the region and the entire ancient Near East, whether or not they speak Hebrew. This way they can understand each other when they buy and sell goods.

Since ancient Israel is such an important trading nation, you are also likely to hear many other languages in the marketplaces as well, everything from ancient Egyptian to Assyrian. Don't worry, you won't be expected to learn all of those languages. Almost everyone you're likely to meet in your time as a tourist will speak some Hebrew.

THE NAME GAME

You may be so familiar with modern American names that you don't even think about what they mean. You have a personal name, or first name, and a family name, or last name. That family name may have an obvious meaning. For instance, Williamson is an abbreviation of William's son. It means that someone in the family history was named William and had a son. Or a name may relate to someone's job in the past. The last name Fisher, for instance, might mean that the family had a noted fisherman somewhere in its ancestry.

In ancient Israel, though, you'll find that people are named differently. Last names in ancient Israel always refer to a child's father's first name. For example, a boy whose father is named Simeon might be called Nathan ben Simeon, meaning Nathan, Simeon's son. Miriam bat Nathan means Miriam, Nathan's daughter. In Hebrew *ben* means "son" or "son of" and *bat* means "daughter"

Handy WORDS & PHRASES

First names in ancient Israel have meanings too. Here are a few samples of Hebrew names and English translations:

Abigail	Father's Joy
Benjamin	Son of the Right Hand (that is, favored or most helpful son)
Beth	Life or Oath of God
David	Friend or Beloved
Deborah	Bee
Isaac	Laughter
Jacob	Favored
Naomi	Beautiful or My Joy
Sarah	Princess
Solomon	Peace

Both the Arab peoples and the people of Iceland also base a person's last name on his or her father's first name. In Arabic the words for "son of" are *bin*, or *ibn*, and "daughter of" is *bint*. In Icelandic the son of a man named Sigurd would have Sigurdsson, "Sigurd's son," for his last name. A daughter's last name would be Sigurdsdotter, "Sigurd's daughter."

or "daughter of." In ancient Israel, it's important to be able to trace a person's ancestry through the father's side of the family. This way of tracing ancestry is known as patrilineal descent.

SCHOOL DAYS

Children in ancient Israel in the time of King Solomon don't go to school—but that doesn't mean they don't get a good education. As soon as they are old enough to talk, youngsters are trained to use their memories. They learn the rules and the traditions of their people and their faith.

When it comes time for a boy to learn to read and write and do basic math, the law states that it's the father's job to educate his son. But if for any reason the father isn't able to do this—if, for instance, he's a traveling merchant—he can hire a tutor instead. There aren't any schoolbooks. The tutor draws the letters of the alphabet on a board, and the student learns to read from it. Most boys begin to read when they are about five or six. Some fathers also see to it that their sons are taught some of the arts as well, such as playing a musical instrument or singing.

Girls usually aren't taught to read or write because they are supposed to grow up to be wives and mothers. Israelites believe that girls won't need to be able to read or write to do their work. But there isn't any actual law against teaching girls, and some fathers teach their daughters as well as their sons. Many girls also play musical instruments and sing.

Don't feel sorry for the children of ancient Israel. Although lessons start when a child is about five or six, and the child is also expected to help out around the house at that age, parents allow their children time to play and just be kids as well.

WRITING

Writing isn't thought to be as important as reading in ancient Israel. This may seem strange to you, but there's a certain wise logic behind the belief. After all, the thinking goes, anyone who can read will be able to read words of wisdom—but only someone who is arrogant will claim to be able to write wisdom. You may see public scribes in the marketplace. They can be hired to write letters and documents for people who aren't sure of their writing ability.

Both the Hebrew and the English alphabets probably started with the one that was used by the group of people called Phoenicians, back in about 1500 B.C.E. Our English alphabet went with the Phoenicians into the Mediterranean and came down to us through Greece to Rome. It's formally called the Latin alphabet, and it is completely different in appearance from written Hebrew. English has twenty-six letters. Hebrew has twenty-two characters.

Also, unlike English, Hebrew is written and read from right to left. An easy way to prepare yourself before your visit to ancient Israel is to find a book written in Hebrew in a bookstore or library. You'll see what a book that reads from "back to front" is like. In ancient Israel, though, most writing is done on scrolls made of vellum (thin, fine leather). Books haven't been invented yet.

This chart compares a few characters in the Phoenician, Hebrew, and Roman alphabets.

Phoenician	Hebrew	Roman
𐤊	א	A
𐤁	ב	B
𐤇	ה	H
𐤌	מ	M
𐤍	נ	N

This engraving is a representation of ancient Jerusalem, including King Solomon's temple at the center of the city. Although the engraving was made in 1492 C.E., it conveys the majesty and sheer size of this teeming metropolis during Solomon's reign.

WHICH CITIES TO VISIT

JERUSALEM

This city is a must-see stop for any traveler to ancient Israel. Not only is Jerusalem the capital of the country, it is certainly one of the most famous cities in the world.

Jerusalem is an old city. It was settled three thousand years before the Israelites arrived in the area. The current king's father, King David, captured Jerusalem from a people called the Jebusites. He rebuilt the city on the southern slope of Mount Moriah and picked it as the capital of his kingdom.

King Solomon has extended Jerusalem north to include the mountain itself. He had the valley between his father's city and the mountain filled in with rock and earth to give Jerusalem room to expand. His own royal palace stands here on the landfill. A great temple, which he also built, graces the summit of Mount Moriah.

Many things are worth seeing in Jerusalem. Your tour might begin with the impressive stone city walls and their watchtowers. The walls encircle the whole city and keep it safe from attack by enemies.

TAKE IT From a Local

Perhaps the best-known story about King Solomon comes from the the Jewish Bible (Old Testament), First Book of Kings Chapter 3.

Two women come before Solomon with a baby that they both claim. Solomon declares that since it is not clear which one is the mother, the baby must be cut in half. One woman cries that she's willing to give up the baby if it isn't hurt—and by her reaction, the wise king knows that she is the true mother.

Jerusalem's streets are narrow, unpaved, and winding, and it's fun to wander down them. Eventually, your walking is bound to take you to one of the city's marketplaces. You can't miss finding one. The sound of music and people shouting and laughing, together with the scents of food and spices, will lead you to it.

Markets are almost always crowded, bustling with people. They are full of farm produce, such as piles of grain and ripe, sweet dates, and crafts, such as beautifully embroidered scarves and fine gold jewelry. Merchants sit under shady awnings, displaying their wares and calling to customers to come and buy. Customers shout back that prices are too high, and loud negotiations over the cost begin. But despite the noise, nobody's really angry. This is just the way of the marketplace.

You probably won't get a chance to visit King Solomon's royal palace, though you'll be able to see its massive walls from the outside. The palace took thirteen years to complete. It is written that the palace is 100 cubits long (a cubit is about 18 inches, which makes the palace about 183 feet long), 50 cubits (75 feet) wide, and 30 cubits (45 feet) high. The reception hall is quite impressive by itself. Its roof is held up by forty-five valuable cedar pillars. It's been said that the hall looks like a cedar forest, so it has been named the House of the Forest. The cedar pillars come from Phoenicia. They are part of the trading agreements between King Solomon and King Hiram of Tyre, who also dealt with Solomon's father, King David. Solomon and Hiram also love to trade riddles. So far, it's said, Solomon has been able to answer every one.

In front of the House of the Forest stands the Porch of Pillars. In front of that is the Hall of Judgment, the royal throne room, and the King's Gate, where Solomon's subjects can meet with him.

Part of the palace has been set aside for King Solomon's many wives and especially for his main wife, who is a princess of Egypt. No one knows exactly how many wives Solomon has. Some claim the number is as high as seven hundred.

The most spectacular sight in Jerusalem has to be the great temple on Mount Moriah. The odds are against your seeing it up close, let alone entering it. So holy a building is not open to casual tourists. Rumor has it that a private staircase of sweet-smelling red sandalwood allows the king to go directly from the palace to the temple.

Even though you won't be allowed to enter the temple, you're sure to be impressed by its size. And you'll be able to see the glow of its beau-

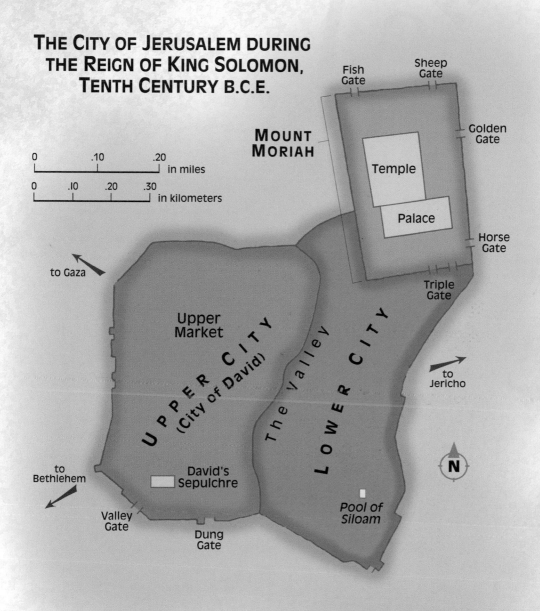

THE CITY OF JERUSALEM DURING THE REIGN OF KING SOLOMON, TENTH CENTURY B.C.E.

Fish Gate

Sheep Gate

MOUNT MORIAH

Golden Gate

Temple

Palace

Horse Gate

0   .10   .20
in miles

0   .10   .20   .30
in kilometers

to Gaza

Triple Gate

Upper Market

U P P E R   C I T Y
(City of David)

The Valley

L O W E R   C I T Y

to Jericho

N

to Bethlehem

David's Sepulchre

Pool of Siloam

Valley Gate

Dung Gate

tiful golden doors even from a distance. It is said that the interior of the temple is covered with gold as well.

Within the temple stands the "great copper sea," an enormous basin set on the figures of twelve bulls. The basin, which is meant for ceremonial washing, is decorated with flower designs pressed into the copper.

Most important of all, the temple houses Israel's holiest object. This is the Ark of the Covenant, a chest containing stone tablets engraved

The Ark of the Covenant (being carried, right) *is one of the holiest objects in all of Judaism. This nineteenth-century painting shows one artist's idea of how the Ark might have looked.*

with the Ten Commandments, the laws given by the Israeli God to the leader Moses in earlier times.

When King Solomon first planned to build the temple, he knew that his own people didn't have the experience for such a complicated project. So he contacted King Hiram of Tyre, the same man who supplied the cedars for Solomon's palace. Solomon knew that Hiram's subjects included skilled architects and craftsmen. Sure enough, Hiram supplied cedar wood, craftsmen, and architects, but even with those expert workers, it still took seven years to complete the temple.

Finally, in 950 B.C.E., a great celebration was held to commemorate the temple's official opening. Some people complain that the architecture looks a little too foreign, with the squared, tapered columns that line the main gate, but all agree that it is a true wonder.

JERICHO

Keep in mind if you go to visit Jericho that you are looking at a unique place, the oldest continuously occupied city in the world. Jericho was originally founded back in about 10,000 B.C.E., and it continues to be a thriving city during King Solomon's reign. Jericho still exists in the modern world.

Jericho is particularly famous for its walls. You may have heard the story of Joshua, an Israelite leader. Joshua is remembered as the one who

In modern Israel, these ruins remind visitors of Jericho's past.

caused the walls of Jericho to tumble down so that the Israelites could conquer the city. New walls surround Jericho, but they, too, may fall someday—the city lies within an earthquake zone.

Jericho is also well worth seeing for its beautiful surroundings. To the east and west are spectacular mountains, and to the south stretches the strange blue of the Dead Sea. There is plenty of water here, some from the nearby Jordan River and some from the runoff of the springs and melting snow on the surrounding mountains. As a result, Jericho is an oasis city, a sea of green in the middle of the desert.

MEGIDDO

This city has a lot of history attached to it. You may have heard of Armageddon, the final battle between good and evil that marks the end of the world in the Christian Bible story. Well, you can visit the actual site of Armageddon. But we're not talking about the end of the world. An actual Battle of Megiddo was the source of the word "Armageddon." The battle took place about four hundred years before King Solomon came to the throne though. The war was between the Egyptians and a people known as the Hittites. During the battle, the old city was completely destroyed. That might be why the idea of a final battle became attached to the name of Megiddo.

Back TO THE Future

Modern archaeologists have been working at Megiddo since the beginning of the twentieth century. The excavations done by the Oriental Institute of the University of Chicago from 1925 to 1939 uncovered evidence of Megiddo's fortifications and gates, its stables, and the impressive, once-secret water systems. The remarkable underground water tunnels that provided the city with water have double-thick walls.

It may have been King Solomon who rebuilt Megiddo, turning it into a fortified government center. That isn't really of interest to most tourists. But the stables for horses and chariots are well worth the visit. There are seventeen barns, plus a large outdoor arena and space for at least 450 horses. Each horse has its own roomy stall. Everything is made out of limestone, so it's fireproof too.

This model of the gate leading into the city of Megiddo shows how well fortified this military settlement is.

What you won't get to see on your visit are Megiddo's secret defenses. It's well known that the king has had a water tunnel and other underground systems built there. In case of an enemy siege, the inhabitants can still obtain water from outside the city walls. No one but the king and his officials know where these systems are.

THE COUNTRYSIDE

You can't truly appreciate ancient Israel without getting out into the countryside. After all, even with all of ancient Israel's trade with the outside world, this is still a land that depends mostly on farming to survive.

All farmers depend on the rain. But in a desert land such as ancient Israel, rain can be scarce. We may think that morning dew is just a wet nuisance. But farmers in ancient Israel depend on every morning's dew to deliver precious moisture to their crops. Some farmers, particularly those who live in the drier areas of the southeast, dig irrigation canals to channel water from rivers and springs to their crops.

But a lack of water isn't the only problem. Hot wind also blows in from the desert. When it blows over farmland, it can suck the moisture right out of the soil and dry up the crops. Insects are a problem too, including the occasional plague of locusts. Locusts, a kind of grasshopper, can devour all the plants in their path. About the only good thing the Israelites have to say about them is that they are edible.

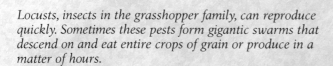

Locusts, insects in the grasshopper family, can reproduce quickly. Sometimes these pests form gigantic swarms that descend on and eat entire crops of grain or produce in a matter of hours.

A farmer also is likely to run into problems with wild animals that want to steal his crops or kill his stock. You'll probably see that many farms have walls around their fields, with sharp thorns on top. Some farmers even have watchtowers, where they and their family members can alternate keeping watch during the growing season. The watcher will

Watchtowers such as this one dot the ancient Israeli landscape.

28

Desert foxes, such as this Blanford's fox, are nocturnal—they sleep during the day and are active at night. Foxes like this one are just one of many threats that watchers in ancient Israel may spot from their watchtowers.

chase off marauding foxes and birds—and every now and then, a human thief trying to steal fruit or a sheep or two.

The most likely crops you will see are grains, such as wheat and barley, flax, and a mix of vegetables, everything from garlic to peppers. Some farmers specialize in fruit trees and have small orchards of pomegranates, dates, and figs. Others grow olive and nut trees or vines for grapes.

Fields often are planted with two or three crops each year, and farmers know about crop rotation. This means alternating the crops planted in a field each season to keep the field more fertile. Often, you'll see a field with growing plants next to one with nothing in it. That's the law. The law states that fields are to lie fallow, or unplanted, every seven years. This is good for the land, which needs to restore itself.

One type of farming you may never have seen before is called terrace farming. This is done in the more mountainous regions, where there isn't much flat land. A farmer starts by building a wall along the lower side of a hill. He then fills in the area between the top of the wall and the hill with

Tech Talk

Humans have grown flax since about 3000 B.C.E. Its stalks can be turned into a fiber (called linen) that can be woven into clothing. Flaxseeds contain oil that can be pressed out and used as fuel. Flaxseed even has a medicinal use. In ancient Israel, and even in modern times, it is used to ease stomachaches.

29

Terraced agricultural fields make farming on hillsides much easier.

soil. This creates a flat, terraced field, which he can then sow with seeds. A series of walls and fields may be constructed up the mountainside.

Farmers often have animals—such as donkeys, mules, and oxen—to help with the heavy work. You may see a farmer plowing a field with a team of oxen or mules. Some farmers also keep small flocks of sheep. Sheep need a shepherd to watch over them. The shepherd is often the farmer's youngest son. King David was a shepherd when he was a boy. He learned to chase away predators with stones hurled from his slingshot. According to a Bible story, he later used his slingshot to kill the giant Philistine warrior Goliath.

Harvest season in ancient Israel begins in Nissan (March–April), with the flax harvest. Next is barley harvest in Iyar (April–May). Then comes wheat in Sivan (May–June), figs and grapes in Elul (August–September), and olives in Tishri (September–October). Everyone in the family joins in the harvest. If you're visiting a farm, you may be asked to help out. Be prepared for hard work.

Grain is harvested with a sickle, a short, curved knife, and then bundled together into a sheaf. Farmers take care not to be too thorough about harvesting every sheaf of grain, every bunch of grapes, or every handful of olives. Something must always be left behind for the poor.

Because there is no refrigeration, farmers have to be careful about storing food. Fruit can be dried, and olives turned into oil. Grapes that aren't eaten or turned into wine can be dried into raisins. Nuts have to be stored in a cool, dry place.

Grain needs special work. The harvested sheaves are taken to a threshing floor, a hard, flat surface in the breeziest spot in the area. Several local farmers may build one threshing floor that is shared by all of them.

First, the farmers separate the grain kernels from the stalks, which is done either by beating them with sticks or by trampling them under animal hooves. Then the grain needs to be winnowed. This means tossing it up in the air so that the lighter chaff, or husks, blow away from the heavier grain. Finally, the grain is run through a sieve to completely separate the grain from bits of chaff and dust. If you visit a farm in the month of Sivan, you may be able to watch the threshers at work.

Grain has to be carefully stored to keep out rot and rodents and insects. It is usually stored as whole kernels, not flour. Flour spoils too quickly. If you see a round structure with openings just below the roof, you're looking at a granary. Farmers usually have their own small granaries to store enough grain for themselves and their families. Most cities have larger granaries that serve as storehouses of food in case of emergencies.

Many farmers will use a scythe (above) *to cut and harvest grain. In Israel and surrounding areas, such as Egypt, oxen or other large animals sometimes help in the threshing process* (right).

MONEY MATTERS

A Spoon for Your Grapes

Coins don't exist in Solomon's kingdom. Most of the time, people simply barter, or trade, for what they want. A man might offer a carved wooden spoon in exchange for a bunch of grapes. But Israelis also use stone or silver weights to determine the value of goods to be traded. This means that scales and honest merchants are important. You put the sack of grain you're buying on one side of the scale, and the

Stone weights help keep bartering fair.

The scale is a common sight in any ancient Israeli marketplace.

merchant puts his marked weights on the other. When the scale is evenly balanced, you know how much the sack weighs and what it is worth. Traveling merchants often carry their own sets of weights, so that they know they won't be cheated.

What about paying taxes? Many people pay with produce, wheat or wine, oil or wool. They may also pay with labor, working for a certain number of days at government construction sites as their tax payment.

POSTCARDS FROM ANCIENT ISRAEL

Don't even try to send a postcard to anyone. Ancient Israel does not have a rapid mail system. An emergency message or one from the king travels by royal chariot. Ordinary messages get delivered from town to town only at the pace of the fastest walker. Visitors are always welcome in small towns, since they bring news of the outside world.

HOW TO GET AROUND

BY LAND

Getting around ancient Israel isn't so easy. There aren't many good roads, except for the main trade routes. One of these trade roads runs from Tyre south through ancient Israel, across the Negev Desert, and on into Egypt. Another one hugs the coast from north of Tyre south through Megiddo and eventually on into Egypt. There are a couple of east-west routes too. One of these runs across ancient Israel through Jericho. But if you just want to get from village to village, you may find only a footpath.

How do you get around ancient Israel? For the most part, you walk. It's common to see someone walking along the road next to a donkey carrying bags of grain or other produce. But if you feel you're not up to a lot of walking, you can hire a riding donkey or a mule, though mules are more expensive. The cost of a horse is beyond the range of most tourists. You may see some mule-drawn wagons on the main roads, and you might be able to hitch a ride on one from a merchant or farmer. Forget about trying to hitch a ride on a chariot, though. Only the government and the military are allowed to travel by chariot.

Most ancient Israelis aren't lucky enough to travel by chariot, but government officials and soldiers can. This Assyrian chariot is similar to the models used by ancient Israeli bigwigs.

Phoenician ships like these three are common in ancient Israeli harbors.

BY WATER

You won't be doing much travel within ancient Israel by water, and if you look at the map, you'll see why. There just isn't enough water, except for the Jordan River, the Sea of Galilee (called Lake Tiberias or Kinneret in modern times), and the Dead Sea. The Dead Sea is so salty that if you want to cross it, you won't even need a boat. You'll float no matter what you do!

On the coast, you'll be able to find ships that sail out into the Mediterranean Sea to Egypt, Greece, and other parts of Europe. King Solomon has also built a major port, Ezion-geber, in the south on the Red Sea. His fleet is manned by Phoenicians, who are master sailors.

Tech Talk

If you've ever gone swimming, you know how easy it is to float. And it's even easier to float in saltwater. You float better in saltwater because the salt and other minerals make saltwater denser, or thicker, than freshwater. The heavier saltwater pushes you up so that you don't sink.

LOCAL CUSTOMS & MANNERS

Much like modern parents, mothers and fathers in ancient Israel had the final word on all matters that took place within the home. This household once belonged to a Jewish priest and his family.

HERO OR TYRANT

In ancient Israel, the father is the head of the family. By law he has the power of life or death over his family. But this doesn't mean that the average husband is—or wants to be— a tyrant. Officially, it's the father who decides who his children can marry and who can be invited into the house. But this doesn't mean that a father won't listen to his son who has fallen in love with the girl next door. And a daughter has the right to say no if she doesn't like the husband her father chooses for her. As for guests, if a woman wants to invite her friend for a chat in the afternoon, it's unlikely that her husband is going to make a fuss about it.

WOMEN'S WORLD

Although ancient Israel is often seen as a man's world, with men holding all the high offices and most of the jobs, women are in charge of running the households. They prepare meals, clean the house, wash the clothes, weave linen and wool, and care for the children.

A few Israelite women also learned to succeed in the outside world. Deborah, who lived about two hundred years before Solomon came to the throne, was a very important figure. She was a prophet and judge, as well as a military leader in Israel's victory over the Canaanites. Jael, a legendary heroine who lived at the same time as Deborah, killed the

Ancient Israeli women have responsibility for domestic tasks, such as kneading and baking bread.

Canaanite military leader Sisera with a well-placed tent peg driven through his skull.

KEEPERS OF WISDOM

Older people are highly respected in ancient Israel. They are seen as the keepers of wisdom and are expected to pass on that wisdom to the younger generation. In Israelite villages, the council of elders sees that things run smoothly.

Ancient Israel has no retirement homes and no Social Security program. But everyone knows that just as the older generation once took care of the young, the younger generation must care for the old. This is one reason why ancient Israelites like large families. Parents can see that it is good to have more helping hands in business or on the farm, and a larger family guarantees more children to help care for the parents when they can no longer work.

TAKE IT from a Local

To every thing there is a season, and a time to every purpose under the heaven . . . .

A time to be born,
and a time to die;
a time to plant,
and a time to pluck up that which
is planted . . . .

A time to weep,
and a time to laugh;
a time to mourn,
and a time to dance . . . .

A time to love,
and a time to hate;
a time of war,
and a time of peace.

—*Ecclesiastes 3*

Local Manners

You'll find that most of the people you meet in ancient Israel will be polite and friendly toward strangers. Like many desert people, they have strong feelings of hospitality. This stems from the time more than two hundred years earlier when the Israelites had left Egypt and were wanderers in the Sinai Desert. In the deep desert, where water is scarce, refusing a person food and drink might well mean condemning him or her to death.

Guests aren't asked any questions, not even their names, since it's not considered polite to pry into someone else's business. In the desert, even an enemy is granted hospitality inside a man's tent. In the law of the desert, hospitality is stronger than the fiercest of feuds.

Hot Hint

A good host makes strangers welcome by washing their feet.

Slavery

Ancient Israelites have slaves, but for the most part, their lot isn't as bad as it is for slaves in other countries. Ancient Israelites don't think that it is right to abuse slaves.

There are two types of slaves. The first group consists of enemies who were captured in battle. Although they become slaves, they aren't

Prisoners of war are often made to do slave labor.

sold in the marketplace. They automatically become servants of the king and other officials. Although slaves aren't treated badly, they can't be freed, either.

The second type of slave provides what can be called temporary slave labor. A man who owes a lot of money might go into slavery as a debt slave, someone who works off what he owes. A debt slave is set free when he pays off his debt in work or after six years of service, whichever comes first.

LOCAL BELIEFS

Most of the people who live in ancient Israel are Jews. They follow the religion of Judaism. Jewish people believe in one God, and they believe that this God has a special relationship with them. Since King Solomon has turned his kingdom into a trading capital, you're also likely to see more than a few people of other faiths and beliefs, as well.

Even in ancient Israel, you should be able to find a few good luck charms. You may see little figures of pregnant women to bring good luck to families wanting children or a *hamesh*, a charm in the shape of a hand for protection.

Handy WORDS & PHRASES

Hamesh is the Hebrew word for "five," and it also means the five fingers of the hand. The Arabs call the amulet in the shape of a hand *hamsa*, which means "five" in Arabic. Israelis may also call it the Hand of Miriam, the sister of Moses. Arabs may call it the Hand of Fatimah, the daughter of Muhammad, who founded their religion, Islam. Either way, the hand amulet is believed to protect its owner from harm.

The Hand of Miriam is an important good luck charm to ancient Israelis.

Horned altars, such as this one in Beersheba, are used to burn incense during the High Holy Days.

HOLIDAYS

Many of the holidays you may witness during your visit to ancient Israel are still celebrated by modern Jews. For instance, these include the High Holy Days of Rosh Hashanah, the New Year's celebration, and Yom Kippur, the Day of Atonement. Yom Kippur is a time when Jewish people repent their sins and ask forgiveness from God and from those they have wronged.

You may be surprised to find that no one in ancient Israel has ever heard about Hanukkah, the Festival of Lights. There's a good reason for this: The historical events behind this holiday haven't happened yet. In fact, they won't happen for about seven hundred years.

MARRIAGE VOWS

People in ancient Israel believe that a full life means getting married and having children. If a woman can't have children, she may even suggest to her husband that he take her maid as a second wife in the hope that the servant will be able to have a child, and the family will have an heir.

In modern times, when a couple becomes engaged, they may or may not get married. In ancient Israel, though, a betrothal—which is the older form of an engagement—is considered very important. As soon as a betrothal is arranged, the marriage is considered official. The couple who is betrothed is legally married, even before the wedding ceremony.

The wedding day is chosen so that it doesn't conflict with a holy day of fasting, since everyone knows there will be lots of eating and celebrating before and after the ceremony. It's unlikely that you, as a tourist, will have a chance to see the wedding, since that's for family and close friends. Although the new husband is expected to lead the family, he is required by holy law to make his wife happy, and both bride and groom expect love from one another.

Even though you may not see the wedding, you may get to see a wedding procession, first as the bride is taken to meet her groom and then,

after the ceremony, as the young couple is led to their new home. You'll know it's a wedding procession because there will be lots of music and singing. People will spread money and grain—the way we throw rice at a modern wedding—before the newly married couple.

DEATH & BEYOND

The ancient Israelites don't believe that death is the end. But they make no claims as to what an afterworld might be like. Instead, they believe that if you lead a good life, you won't have to worry about what might come afterward.

In this time of King Solomon, people are just beginning to build mausoleums, or large, elegant tombs that look almost like houses. Most people, though, still follow the old custom of burying a corpse in a linen shroud, without a coffin, so that the body may return to the earth more quickly. Funerals are performed very soon after a person's death, mostly because of the hot climate.

This mausoleum belongs to a member of the Sanhedrin. During Solomon's time, the Sanhedrin was a high court of seventy-one wise men who made decisions about Jewish laws.

WHAT TO WEAR

Linen, a cloth woven from the fibers of the flax plant, is one of the two fabrics used for clothing in ancient Israel.

LINEN OR WOOL?

Just as in the modern world, what you wear in ancient Israel depends on who you are and how much you can afford to spend on clothing. If you're visiting a farm, you'll see that farmers don't bother with any fancy wear. Since they spend so much time working out in the hot sun, they wear as little as possible, usually no more than a loincloth or a simple tunic woven of undyed wool.

Almost everyone wears ankle-length tunics. Only the very poor or those who are in mourning go barefoot. Everyone else wears leather sandals.

You won't find much variety in the fabrics that ordinary people wear. There's linen and there's wool, and that's pretty much it. Silk hasn't made its way into ancient Israel yet, and cotton is unknown.

Of course, linen can be woven with very fine thread, the way the Egyptians do it, so that it's as soft as silk and nearly transparent. And wool can be woven in all sorts of thicknesses, too, from heavy weaves for winter to lightweight ones that are comfortable even in the summer. Different types of woolen outfits can be worn comfortably year-round.

Dyers add color to the fabrics. People like colorful clothing, so you may see someone with a robe that's striped red and yellow or dyed a rich blue. Embroidery worked in bright threads also adds color to the sleeves, collars, and hems of people's clothing.

Many people cinch in their tunic with a sash of a different color. Since tunics have no pockets, men and women hang their purses and small tools, such as knives or combs, from their sashes.

On colder days, a well-dressed man or woman might add a mantle, or cloak, of heavier wool. This might be dyed the same color as the tunic, but it might also be dyed a bold, contrasting color or even in stripes. On a journey, the heavier mantle may be used as a blanket or bedding.

You'll find that styles of dress are more elegant in the big cities. In Jerusalem, for instance, you might see a wealthy woman wearing a many-colored tunic of linen so fine that it looks like silk. She will wear

Although clothing is simple, it need not be boring. Stripes and patterns are popular among the fashionable and wealthy in both Egypt (right) and Israel.

golden earrings and bracelets, anklets, and maybe even a nose ring. Her head will probably be covered with a richly embroidered linen veil. From her sash will be hanging an ivory box that holds her cosmetics or a vial of her favorite perfume. Men don't dress quite so elegantly, although they, too, will wear tunics of many colors and gold ornaments, particularly gold rings.

HAIR

Both men and women in ancient Israel like to wear their hair long, although women often cover their hair with scarves or veils. Men can sometimes be seen wearing linen turbans.

In ancient Israel, people wear their hair straight. Men grow beards as soon as they are old enough, but it's not considered proper for a man to waste time curling or styling his beard or hair.

SIDE TRIP TRIVIA

Unlike in Israel, people in other countries of the ancient Middle East curl their hair and wear it in long braids or ringlets. Men also curl and style their beards.

BEAUTY

You will probably notice that many women in ancient Israel use some kind of makeup. They have eyeliner made out of a black mineral called kohl. Kohl is still in use as an eyeliner in the modern world. Another type of eye shadow in ancient Israel is made out of a powdered green mineral, called malachite.

Women kept their kohl eyeliner in ornately carved boxes.

46

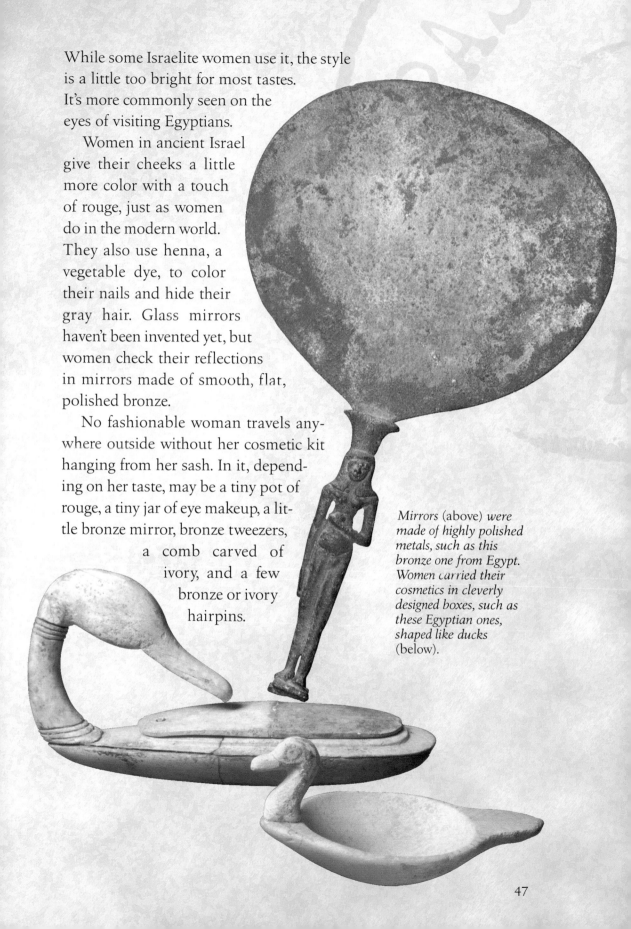

While some Israelite women use it, the style is a little too bright for most tastes. It's more commonly seen on the eyes of visiting Egyptians.

Women in ancient Israel give their cheeks a little more color with a touch of rouge, just as women do in the modern world. They also use henna, a vegetable dye, to color their nails and hide their gray hair. Glass mirrors haven't been invented yet, but women check their reflections in mirrors made of smooth, flat, polished bronze.

No fashionable woman travels anywhere outside without her cosmetic kit hanging from her sash. In it, depending on her taste, may be a tiny pot of rouge, a tiny jar of eye makeup, a little bronze mirror, bronze tweezers, a comb carved of ivory, and a few bronze or ivory hairpins.

Mirrors (above) were made of highly polished metals, such as this bronze one from Egypt. Women carried their cosmetics in cleverly designed boxes, such as these Egyptian ones, shaped like ducks (below).

WHAT TO SEE & DO

ENTERTAINMENT

Ancient Israel isn't a sports-minded country. But that doesn't mean you won't find other entertainments.

Wandering through any of the marketplaces in ancient Israel is always fun. A market in ancient Israel is a great place to try out your bartering skills, since nothing has a fixed price. When a merchant names a value for an item, you are expected to offer a lower one. Then the merchant comes down a bit, and you go up a bit until you both agree on the price of the item. Don't expect to be better than the local people at bargaining though. They have had years of experience!

Another entertainment is music. King David was a musician and composer, and his son, the current king, shares his late father's musical talents. So there are plenty of performances both at court and in the marketplace. Performers sing and play musical instruments.

TAKE IT from a Local

Praise him with trumpet sound; praise him with lute and harp! Praise him with timbrel and dance; praise him with strings and pipe! Praise him with sounding cymbals; praise him with loud clashing cymbals!

—*King David*
Psalms 150: 3–5

A female musician taps out a rhythm on a tambourine.

Some of the instruments you're most likely to hear are the lyre, a type of harp, and the timbrel, a type of small drum. You'll also hear the sistrum, a type of rattle, and several kinds of flutes.

Still another form of entertainment is storytelling. In the cities, you're likely to find storytellers in any marketplace. In the villages, some of the village elders may tell tales. These range from religious stories to wonder tales, or the traditional "once upon a time" stories.

Musicians play tunes upon lyres (top), *sistrums* (middle), *and flutes* (bottom).

WHERE TO STAY

Inns are often made of stone taken from surrounding areas.

PUBLIC ACCOMMODATIONS

Every city in ancient Israel has its share of inns. You can also find inns along every major road. What the inn will look like depends on where it is. If it's located in the mountains, the walls are almost certainly going to be made of stone, since stone is abundant there. But if the inn is down in the desert, its walls are going to be made of mud brick instead, since there's not much stone along the desert roads.

An inn, like any other house in ancient Israel, is probably going to have a flat roof made of wooden beams and brush. A coating of clay makes it waterproof and sturdy. The rooms will be built around a central courtyard, where the inn's oven will stand. Don't expect to find a door to your room. There aren't likely to be any. Instead, there will be a curtain to give you a bit of privacy.

Don't expect a private bath, either. Bathtubs are almost unheard of in ancient Israel, except in the homes of the very rich or in the royal palace. Water is very valuable—and very expensive—in a desert land. You'll be expected to bathe, or at least to wash your hands, feet, and face, in a basin. The usual soap is a vegetable mixture that takes off the dirt but is rather harsh on the skin. A good inn will provide oil for a visitor to soothe skin irritated by the soap and by the dry desert weather.

PRIVATE HOMES

The people of ancient Israel believe strongly in the laws of hospitality. This means that if you're invited to visit someone's house, you'll truly be made welcome.

The typical house in ancient Israel is built like the inns, in a square around an open courtyard. Like the inns, the home has walls of stone or mud brick, depending on its location. Each family has its oven in the courtyard, where smoke can escape easily without choking the household. Here also are querns, the stones used to grind wheat or barley into flour.

Most families live in a four-room house. When you enter one of these houses, you'll see that there is one room to the left of the central courtyard, one room to the right of the courtyard, and one long room beyond the courtyard. The courtyard itself is considered the fourth room. Of course, if a family wants more rooms, they can build a wall across one of the four existing ones.

This model of the layout of an ancient Israeli home shows how rooms were built around a central courtyard. This particular building has an additional two rooms at the front of the home and two enclosed spaces at the back.

The remains of these homes in Der Samet have enclosed sleeping areas on their roofs.

In most houses, a staircase leads up to the roof. Because it's usually cooler up there, thanks to breezes, people like to spend time on the roof. There's often a railing around the edge so that no one will fall off.

In the chilly winters, people stay indoors and heat their homes with the cooking fire. The wood of the white broom plant is a favorite fuel. The embers of the white broom stay hot for a long time. They provide an even, steady heat that's good for cooking or baking. Also, the embers can be easily fanned back into flame. People in ancient Israel light their fires by striking a flint or by rubbing two sticks together.

Poorer people have houses with only one room, plus a stairway to the roof, which becomes a second room. People live on the roof in summer, eating and sleeping there in the cooler air.

Cities such as Jerusalem have mansions, too. You may or may not get a chance to see the inside of one of these houses. They have many more rooms than the simple four. Some of them have two floors instead of just one. Some of them even have true basements as well. Cisterns, tanks or vats for storing rainwater, are found in the basement. The family's bathtub might be there, too. Mansion walls are often decorated with painted designs or with stucco plastering worked into geometric patterns.

The furniture people own reflects their wealth. In an ordinary home, you may see nothing more than a table and a chair or two made of wood. In fact, the family may not even have a true table, just a slightly raised work area. People don't usually use the table for dining. In many homes, the family simply sits on cushions or mats on the floor and eats from a central platter of food. In King Solomon's palace, however, it is said that royal feasts are spread on tables with legs.

Handy Words & Phrases

The Hebrew word *keesay* can mean "chair," "seat," or "throne." Take your choice.

In an ordinary house, the chairs will probably just be stools or folding stools. Some people prefer regular chairs, with armrests and footrests. These may be made entirely of wood, or they may have a wooden frame with woven cords to make the seat and back. There aren't any upholstered chairs in ancient Israel. King Solomon, of course, has a true throne with armrests. The throne is inlaid with ivory carvings and plated with gold. It is said that the throne is flanked by carved lions and that it's raised six steps from the throne room floor.

There usually isn't a real bed in an ordinary home. People sleep on a few mats piled on the floor or maybe on a separate raised platform.

In a wealthier house, you can expect to find a real bed, piled high with pillows. The pillows are often made of goatskins stuffed with feathers or soft wool. A royal bed, such as one in King Solomon's palace, might be built of ivory, with colored linen sheets from Egypt, scented with cinnamon and other spices.

TAKE IT from a Local

I have decked my couch with coverings, colored spreads of Egyptian linen; I have perfumed my bed with myrrh, aloes, and cinnamon.

—*Proverbs 7: 16–17*

Pottery cooking and food storage vessels are made in all sizes. These vessels come from a period following Solomon's rule but are quite similar to those used during his reign.

In most houses, you will find different sizes and shapes of cooking pots and storage jars. You may also find a loom and such ordinary things as a broom and lamps fueled with olive oil. The oil lamp is the only type of indoor lighting known in ancient Israel.

When you stay in a family's home, just as in an inn, don't expect a separate bathroom. In fact, the family will probably expect you to conserve water as much

An oil lamp

as possible. The only way to get water is to carry it in heavy buckets from the village well or a nearby stream. You'll probably be given some rough vegetable soap to wash with and some oil to soothe your skin. In the wealthiest of homes, however, you'll find fine skin creams containing rich vegetable oils, milk, and honey, with aromatic flowers added to provide a nice scent.

There's one more difference between the houses of the ordinary people and those of the wealthy. The wealthy families live on the west side of town so that the breezes blowing in from the Mediterranean can cool their houses. The poorer families are stuck living on the eastern side of town, where they get less breeze and more dust from the desert soil.

WHAT TO EAT

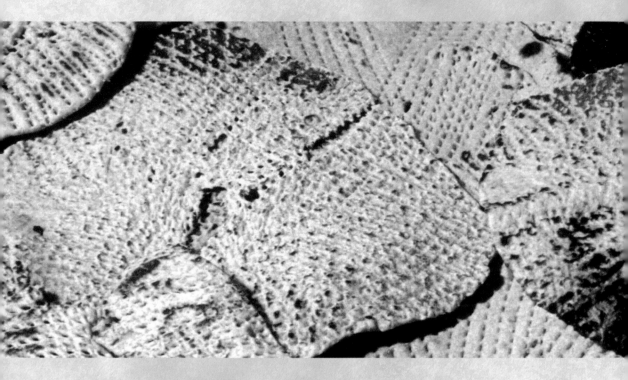

In ancient Israel, people usually eat only two meals a day. While no one's going to stop you from eating whenever you're hungry, the Israelites have a late-morning meal, which is a little like our brunch, and dinner, eaten early in the evening, often before sundown.

You won't have to worry about whether you'll be able to eat well during your visit to ancient Israel. A wide variety of good food can be found in the markets and inns.

THE STAFF OF LIFE

The most basic staple of everyone's diet is bread. You may see two kinds, depending on the time of year. The first, which in modern times can be seen in supermarkets around the Jewish holiday of Passover, is matzah. This is unleavened bread, or bread that has no yeast to make it rise. It was eaten by the Jewish people after they escaped from Egypt in ancient times. It is still baked during Passover to commemorate that long-ago event. Matzah is made of wheat flour and water mixed together into

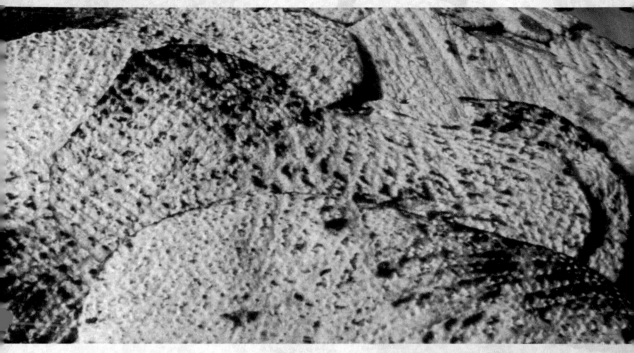

Matzah, a crackerlike form of bread, is eaten at Passover.

dough, then flattened out and baked. Sometimes salt or honey is added to the dough to give the matzah a sharper or sweeter flavor.

The second type of bread is made of barley flour. It is usually made fresh every day. That isn't as easy as it sounds. First, the barley grains have to be ground into flour by hand, usually between two stones. Then water and yeast are added to the barley flour, and it's all mixed together and kneaded into dough. A wealthy household or an inn might have its own earthenware oven, which can be heated to baking temperature by a wood fire burning in a space underneath it. But many families can't afford the expense of an oven and extra fuel, so they take their dough to the local baker for baking.

People also have other ways of preparing bread. Loaves are not only baked in an oven, they also can be fried in a pan. Matzah is sometimes baked in the old-fashioned way of desert nomads, who spread the dough on stones that have been heated in a fire.

Wheat and barley flour are sometimes mixed together with beans and lentils and baked to make a really healthy loaf. People in ancient

Israel don't grow oats, but they make a type of porridge, like oatmeal, that is made out of boiled ground wheat.

WHERE'S THE MEAT?

One thing you won't be able to find during your visit is a steak, for a very good reason. There are few cows in ancient Israel. Cattle have to be imported from beyond the Jordan River, and they are very expensive. Geese and other poultry are imported from Egypt, and they are just as expensive. In fact, most people don't eat meat every day. Sheep and goats are too valuable to kill for food, since they are also sources of milk, wool, and hair. But occasionally you'll find mutton, which is the meat of old sheep, on the menu.

Instead of meat, you will almost always be able to find some good fish to eat. If you happen to be near either the Mediterranean Sea or a major river such as the Jordan, you'll be able to enjoy fish right out of the water. Otherwise, the fish that you get might have been pickled to preserve it. Don't be afraid to try it. Pickled herring is a delicacy.

People in ancient Israel, as well as in the modern Near Eastern world, roast and eat insects such as locusts. These critters are rich in protein and have a nutty flavor.

This wall painting shows fishers hauling enormous catches out of the waters surrounding ancient Israel.

Sheep and goats roam the countryside together. Both are valued for their milk and for the products that can be made from their milk.

Remember those sheep and goats? Thanks to them, you'll be able to find all sorts of cheeses, plain or with herbs added for flavoring. You may even develop a taste for sheep or goat's milk.

Want an omelet? Try one made of wild bird eggs. It won't taste the same as one made from domestic hen eggs, but it won't taste bad, either.

FOODS TO TRY,
at your own risk

— Roasted Locust. Scientists are beginning to think that the ancient Israelites had the right idea. One hundred grams of cricket—which is related to the locust—contains 121 calories, 13 grams of protein, and only 5.5 grams of fat, as well as a lot of good vitamins and minerals. One hundred grams of beef has more protein—about 23.5 grams—but it also has 288 calories and 21 grams of fat.

Foods to Try

— Barley bread

— Bird's egg omelet

— Date and almond candy

— Matzah with honey

— Pickled fish with onions

— Vegetable stew

Eat Your Veggies

The people of ancient Israel like to eat their vegetables. They make several different kinds of vegetable stews with beans, peas, onions, and whatever else is in season. You're also likely to see such fresh vegetables as lettuce and beets, as well as fresh fruits such as dates and pomegranates.

Almost everyone uses olive oil for cooking, and you're sure to see plenty of salt from the Dead Sea. A nice selection of herbs, such as

Dried fruits, such as dates, apricots, and figs, are a tasty treat in ancient Israel.

Olives and olive oil are present in every ancient Israeli kitchen.

coriander, mint, and thyme, grow wild in ancient Israel and can be gathered in the fields. So can garlic and wild onion.

But suppose you have a sweet tooth. Sugar is not available in ancient Israel. But you'll be able to find an assortment of tasty honey cakes and a candy that's made out of dates, honey, and almonds.

As a tourist, you're not likely to get an invitation to eat at the royal palace. But those who've eaten there say that King Solomon sets a lavish table, complete with golden plates.

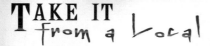

TAKE IT from a Local

King Solomon's palace houses a lot of people. We know from the Tanach that the royal household's provisions for just one day are

— Thirty measures of fine flour

— Threescore [sixty] measures of semolina [another kind of wheat flour]

— Thirty fat oxen

— Twenty oxen out of the pastures

— One hundred sheep

— Deer

— Gazelles

— Fatted Fowl

—*I KINGS 4:22–23*

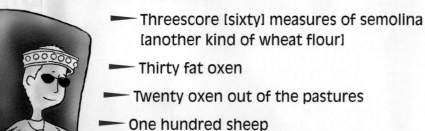

WHERE TO FIND SOUVENIRS

ARTS, CRAFTS, & OTHER DELIGHTS

As you explore Jerusalem or other Israelite cities, you are sure to find marketplaces. But you are also sure to come across squares within each city that hold artisans' shops. Keep your eyes open, because you never know what wonders you might discover.

Maybe you'll get to watch a goldsmith at work. He'll melt down a gold nugget in a closed crucible, a kind of container, so that not a scrap of the precious metal will be lost. Then he'll pour the melted gold carefully into a mold or beat it out with a tiny hammer into fine golden wires to make delicate filigree jewelry.

You may also get to watch a jeweler working with gemstones. Although ancient Israel doesn't have many native gems, gemstones are imported from Egypt and Asia. You might see the jeweler making bracelets of rubies and sapphires or topaz and amethyst. These are probably going to cost more than a tourist can afford, but you might be able to buy jewelry made from Mediterranean coral or pearls.

A jeweler shapes gems by filing them gently with a rough stone, smoothing them with

Gold and gemstone jewelry (left) is crafted in all major cities from stones such as topaz, amethyst, and many others (above).

sand, then polishing them with soft wool. If he wants to turn a gemstone into a bead, he'll use a bow drill, a tool that drills a hole in the stone. The string of the bow is wound about the drill, then pulled and pushed to make the drill spin at high speed. Eventually, this tool drills a hole through the gemstone so that it can be strung on a thread.

Another artisan you might see at work is the ivory carver, who works with ivory or bone. He may be an Israelite, but he's more likely to be an Egyptian or Phoenician, who have been skilled in the art for much longer than the people of ancient Israel. An ivory carver's tools are like those of the jeweler, including the bow drill. Ivory can be worked into jewelry, and you'll probably see ivory beads, earrings, and pendants. Ivory is also made into elegant little perfume bottles, combs, and inlays on furniture, such as carved ivory panels inset into the arms of a chair or the head of a bed.

Ivory vessels, such as this one carved in the shape of a pomegranate, are prized possessions in ancient Israel.

Best Buys

- Gold and silver jewelry
- Ivory and bone carvings
- Embroidered tunics and sashes
- Lyres and other musical instruments
- Pottery bowls and oil lamps
- Copper jewelry and cooking pots

You'll also see a good deal of copper in the markets. Copper is hammered into pots and pans or worked into jewelry. With the help of Phoenician workers, who are experienced in such things, King Solomon has set up a major copper mining operation near his Red Sea seaport of Ezion-geber. In fact, copper is one of ancient Israel's main exports. Since the refinery is right by the seaport, it's easy for merchants to set sail for Arabia or Africa with copper ore and ingots (blocks of pure copper) for trade.

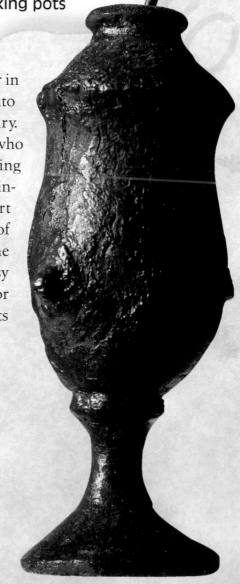

Copper is used to make items such as cosmetics jars. Look for copper trinkets in the market!

HOW TO STAY SAFE & HEALTHY

Garlic is often prescribed to treat common ailments.

TAKE SOME GARLIC & CALL ME IN THE MORNING

Should you need a doctor, you might be startled to learn that he prescribes garlic for internal problems and honey for wounds. Don't worry. Garlic really does have many healing properties and may even lower blood pressure. Honey, which is also used by ancient Egyptian physicians, has some wonderful wound-healing properties, including fighting off infection.

HOLD ONTO YOUR BELONGINGS & BEWARE OF BANDITS

In the cities, you will find crimes such as theft and robbery. In the marketplace, keep a hand on your valuables at all times, since any crowded area with lots of distractions is a great place for pickpockets to work. There won't be any street gangs to worry you. But streetlights don't exist, either, so you won't want to go out after dark.

You can get into real danger on the roads. The first problem comes from the land itself. If you're traveling alone, know something about wilderness survival. You already know not to go off into the Negev Desert alone. But even on a walk from village to village, carry enough water with you and keep your head covered. That's a fierce desert sun up in that beautifully clear, blue sky. The mountain paths beneath your feet can be tricky, and if you break your ankle, you'll have no way to call for help.

Humans might be dangerous, too. There's a good reason for the walls around the cities: ancient Israel has enemies, such as the Canaanites, who also live in the region. Recently, King Solomon had to go to war against the city-state of Hamath, which lies in the northern part of his kingdom, to secure his northern border. He needed to secure it because

IMPORTANT
Safety Tip

There's no real reason to be out at night. Every honest person is already at home, and you won't encounter night concerts or late shopping hours to keep you out after dark.

67

north of it is Aram, the territory of the unfriendly King Rezon. Hamath gave in very easily.

King Solomon has also built a series of fortified cities around his kingdom. Megiddo, Hazor, and Dan are examples of the kind of fortified cities that are flourishing during Solomon's reign. In the Negev Desert, the king has built the military outpost of Tadmor. It also serves as a commercial site, since it stands at the crossroads of two major trade routes. The people can take pride in the fact that, although Solomon has a well-equipped army of fourteen hundred chariots and twelve thousand horsemen, the peace he has established holds. His army has never had to fight a major war.

But no one can be certain that the northern region is absolutely secure. Some raiders who have never accepted the peace may still be out there. Bandits may hide out in the mountains too, and they are difficult to catch. They would love to rob and kill lone travelers who grow careless.

This model of the sturdy, stone gate that protects the military outpost of Hazor shows how serious ancient Israelis are about protecting their country!

As for any desert travels, if you do decide to take a trip into the desert, your best choice is to go with an established caravan of merchants and their pack animals. If you can't find one leaving when you want to travel, a guide may offer his services. Check out any guide with the authorities before you go anywhere with him. You want to be sure that he's not a robber or a fake. The middle of the Negev Desert is no place to discover that your guide doesn't know where to find water or how to get back to civilization.

LAW & ORDER

King Solomon has recently divided his kingdom into twelve political districts. Each district has a governor so that everyone can be ruled—and taxed—fairly. Two of the governors are married to two of the king's daughters, so you can be sure that they are honest men.

The king, of course, is at the head of the government. But Solomon has also set up a cabinet, or a group of advisers. The cabinet members include Zabud, the prime minister, who is also the king's friend; Benaiah, the commander in chief of the army; Elihoreph and Ahijah, brothers and chief scribes; and Adoniram, the head of the treasury. Chiefs direct building projects, and officials oversee the governors of each political district.

Ambassadors, or official representatives from other countries, also come to Jerusalem. King Solomon has been careful to keep up the ties of friendship with King Hiram of Tyre that his father began. Solomon has also kept up good relations with other lands, often through royal marriages. The most important of these is the alliance Solomon made between ancient Israel and Egypt, which is one of the largest and best known of ancient Israel's neighbors. The alliance was made more secure by King Solomon's marriage to a daughter of the Egyptian pharaoh. In fact, Gezer, which is one of Solomon's fortress cities, was originally Egyptian. It was given to the king by Egypt as part of the marriage contract.

Ancient Israel follows the king's laws, and every city or large village has a judge who was sent there by Solomon and is responsible to the king. But ancient Israel also follows the Jewish code of law, the laws of Moses. Judges and priests interpret the law for each case and write down their findings. Teachers and experts in the law serve as lawyers in both ordinary and religious cases.

WHO'S WHO IN ANCIENT ISRAEL

KING DAVID

King David united the loose group of tribes of Israel into a nation by conquering Jerusalem and turning it into a religious center for all Israelites. As a young man, he won fame by killing Goliath, the giant Philistine warrior, with his slingshot. David was a poet and a musician, and by tradition, he is credited as the author of many of the psalms in the Bible. He died about 962 B.C.E.

DEBORAH

Two centuries before Solomon, Deborah was a prophet, judge, and military leader in Israel. She played a major role in Israel's victories over its enemies in the 1100s B.C.E.

HIRAM I OF TYRE

King Hiram (ca. 969–936 B.C.E.) is the rich and powerful ruler of Phoenicia, a kingdom north and west of ancient Israel. Hiram had been an ally of King David and continues the alliance with David's son, Solomon. He and Solomon are said to have traded riddles along with goods. Hiram, or Ahiram, was a popular name for Phoenician rulers.

QUEEN OF SHEBA

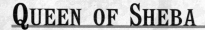

The Queen of Sheba may or may not have existed. She may have been the ruler of Saba, a kingdom in what became southern Saudi Arabia. A folk belief says that she was so in awe of King Solomon's wisdom that she paid him a visit to test him. While there is no archaeological or biblical proof, it is true that Israel under Solomon did trade with Saba.

KING SOLOMON

Solomon was born in 1035 B.C.E. and has reigned as king of Israel since 968 B.C.E. He inherited the throne from his father, King David. Solomon is famous for having built the region's first temple, which made Jerusalem into a great religious center. Solomon also turned Israel into a trading power, making alliances with such countries as Egypt and Phoenicia. He is credited as the author of many songs and proverbs and is famous for his wisdom. His reign is called Israel's golden age.

PREPARING FOR THE TRIP

BAKE SOME MATZAH

(Note: You might want to ask an adult for help.) What you'll need:

> 2 cups flour (bread flour, not cake flour)
> 1 teaspoon salt
> ½ cup milk or water
> ¼ cup olive oil
> 2 tablespoons honey (optional)

What you'll do:
1. Preheat the oven to 375°F.
2. Use one spoon to mix the flour and salt in a bowl.
3. Use a second spoon to mix the milk or water, oil, and honey in a separate bowl. Add to the flour mixture. Mix it all up with your hands.
4. Place the dough on a flat, floured surface. Knead it by patting it out and folding it back on itself a few times.
5. Separate the dough into several 5-inch circles or squares. Flatten the circles or squares of dough until they are about ½ inch thick. Prick some holes in each piece with a fork. Put the flat pieces of dough on a cookie sheet.

The Hebrews move to Egypt
ca. 1600 B.C.E.

The Hebrews leave Egypt and enter the Sinai Desert.
ca. 1400–1300 B.C.E.

The fall of Jericho's walls and the beginning of Israel
ca. 1300–1200 B.C.E.

1600 B.C.E.   1400 B.C.E.   1200 B.C.E. . . . .

6. Bake for 20 minutes.

7. Remove from the oven. Turn off the oven.

8. Let the matzah cool on the cookie sheet.

Enjoy!

MAKE AN OIL LAMP

(Note: You might want to ask an adult for help.). What you'll need:

> Modeling clay
> Olive oil, or other cooking oil
> 3 or 4 inches of cotton cord
> Matches

What you'll do:

1. Flatten a piece of clay and use your fingers to shape it into a circle or oval.

2. Turn up the edges of the clay to form a bowl.

3. Pinch one part of the edge of the bowl so that it's a little higher than the rest and forms a lip.

4. Carefully pour ¼ inch of oil into the clay bowl. Place the cotton cord in the oil, but leave one end to hang about 1 inch over the edge of the lip. With a match, light the end of the cord that is hanging over the edge of the lamp.

5. Be sure to blow out the flame when you are finished with your lamp.

The Period of the Judges, when the judge and prophet Deborah lived.

ca. 1200–1050 B.C.E.

The Philistines defeat the Israelite tribes in battle and occupy Israel.

ca. 1050 B.C.E.

. . .1200 B.C.E.

1050 B.C.E.

GLOSSARY

Aramaic: the trading language of ancient Israel. This is also the language of the Aramaeans of ancient Syria.

Canaanites: inhabitants of Israel who were defeated by the Israelites arriving from Egypt

crop rotation: changing the crop planted in a field each season

hamesh: a good luck charm in the shape of a hand

irrigation: watering of crops by directing river water or well water to fields through a series of ditches or trenches

fallow: unplanted

Philistines: a people living in Israel who fought the Israelites and eventually were defeated by them

quern: a stone used to grind grain into flour

refinery: a building where raw materials are turned into useable products

shroud: a cloth used to wrap a body for burial

sistrum: a musical instrument, similar to a rattle

Tanach: the Jewish Holy Scriptures, including the Five Books of Moses

terrace farming: a type of farming in a mountain area, in which a farmer builds a field between a wall and a hillside

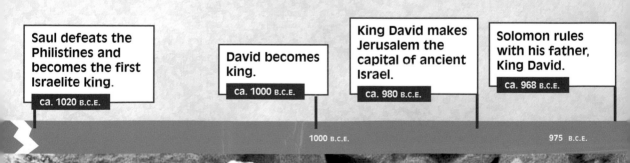

Saul defeats the Philistines and becomes the first Israelite king.
ca. 1020 B.C.E.

David becomes king.
ca. 1000 B.C.E.

King David makes Jerusalem the capital of ancient Israel.
ca. 980 B.C.E.

Solomon rules with his father, King David.
ca. 968 B.C.E.

1000 B.C.E.

975 B.C.E.

PRONUNCIATION GUIDE

Aramaic	ahr-uh-MAY-ihk
Canaanites	KAY-nuh-nyts
Ezion-geber	EE-zee-ahn GEE-bar
Galilee	GAL-uh-lee
Goliath	goh-LY-ahth
Hamath	HAY-mahth
hamesh	HAY-mehsh
Jebusites	JEHB-yoo-syts
Jericho	JEHR-uh-koh
Jerusalem	jehr-OO-sehl-ehm
malachite	ma-luh-KYT
matzah	MAHT-zah
Megiddo	meh-GIH-doh
Mount Moriah	mount mohr-Y-ah
Philistine	FIHL-eh-steen
Phoenicia	fih-NEE-shah
quern	KWERN
sistrum	SIHS-trihm
Tanach	TAH-nahk
Tyre	TIRE

Solomon becomes king.
ca. 960 B.C.E.

Solomon builds the first temple in ancient Israel.
ca. 950 B.C.E.

End of Solomon's reign
ca. 927 B.C.E.

960 B.C.E.

900 B.C.E.

FURTHER READING & WEBSITES

Books

Day, Nancy. *Your Travel Guide to Ancient Egypt.* Minneapolis: Runestone Press, 2001.

Farb, Peter. *Land, Wildlife and Peoples of the Bible.* New York: HarperCollins, 1967.

Goldstein, Margaret J. *Israel in Pictures.* Minneapolis: Lerner Publications Company, 2004.

Gresko, Marcia. *Israel.* Minneapolis: Carolrhoda Books, Inc., 2000.

Moorey, P. R. S. *The Making of the Past: The Biblical Lands.* New York: Peter Bedrick Books, 1991.

Motyer, Stephen. *Bible Atlas.* New York: DK Publishing, 2001.

Slavik, Diane. *Daily Life in Ancient and Modern Jerusalem.* Minneapolis: Runestone Press, 2001.

Tubb, Jonathan N. *Eyewitness: Bible Lands.* New York: DK Publishing, 2000.

Websites

Internet Ancient History Sourcebook: Israel
<http://www.fordham.edu/halsall/ancient/asbook06.html>
An excellent starting point for research, this list of web links covers everything from culture and history of ancient Israel to modern views of this time period.

The Jewish Museum in the City of New York
<http://www.jewishmuseum.org>
Get a quick preview of exhibitions at this renowned museum of art and artifacts. Detailed descriptions of past, present, and future exhibitions are included.

A Virtual Museum of Ancient Israel
<http://rims.k12.ca.us/ancient_hebrews>
This online museum details aspects of ancient Israeli daily life, beliefs, and more. The site is illustrated with paintings and photographs.

Women's Life in Ancient Israel
<http://www.womenintheancientworld.com>
Learn about the status, role, and daily life of women in ancient Israel. This site also explores the lives of women living in ancient Egypt, Rome, Athens, and Babylonia.

BIBLIOGRAPHY

Bennett Jr, Boyce M. and David H. Scott. *Harper's Encyclopedia of Bible Life*. Rev. ed. New York: Harper & Row, 1978.

Boccaccini, Gabriele. *Roots of Rabbinic Judaism*. Grand Rapids, MI: Eerdemans Publishing Company, 2002.

De Vaux, Roland. *Ancient Israel: Its Life and Institutions*. Grand Rapids, MI: Eerdemans Publishing Company, 1997.

Isserlin, B. S. J. *The Israelites*. Minneapolis: The Fortress Press, 2001.

Kuntz, J. Kenneth. *The People of Ancient Israel*. New York: Harper & Row, 1974.

McNutt, Paula. *Reconstructing the Society of Ancient Israel*. Louisville, KY: Westminster John Knox Press, 1999.

Meilsheim, D. *The World of Ancient Israel*. New York: Tudor Publishing, Inc., 1973.

Moorey, P. R. S. *The Making of the Past: The Biblical Lands*. New York: Peter Bedrick Books, 1991.

Perdue, Leo G., et al. *Families in Ancient Israel*. Louisville, KY: Westminster John Knox Press, 1997.

Redford, Donald B. *Egypt, Canaan, and Israel in Ancient Times*. Princeton, NJ: Princeton University Press, 1997.

Rogerson, J. W. *Chronicle of the Old Testament Kings: The Reign-by-Reign Record of the Rulers of Ancient Israel*. London and New York: Thames and Hudson, 1999.

Sanders, Nancy I. *Old Testament Days*. Chicago: Chicago Review Press, 1999.

Shanks, Hershel, ed. *Ancient Israel: From Abraham to the Roman Destruction of the Temple*. Washington, D.C.: Biblical Archaeology Society, 1999.

Vos, Howard F. *Nelson's New Illustrated Bible Manners & Customs*. Nashville: Thomas Nelson, Inc., 1999.

INDEX

ABOUT THE AUTHOR

Josepha Sherman is a professional author, folklorist, and editor. A former assistant curator for the Metropolitan Museum of Art in New York City, she has a degree in Ancient Near Eastern Archaeology. Among her titles for younger readers are *Bill Gates: Computer King*, *Deep Space Observational Satelites*, *Welcome to the Rodeo*, and numerous others. She is a winner of the Compton Crook Award for best first fantasy novel and has been nominated numerous times for the Nebula Award. She lives in New York City.

Acknowledgments for Quoted Material: pp. 8, 38 Roy B. Chamberlin and Herman Feldman, *The Dartmouth Bible* (Boston: Houghton Mifflin, 1950); pp. 49, 54, Educational Heritage: *The World of the Bible, Book IV* (Yonkers, NY: Educational Heritage, Inc., 1959).

Photo Acknowledgments
The images in this book are reproduced with the permission of: Courtesy of the Israel Ministry of Tourism, pp. 2, 6–7, 10, 12; Laura Westlund, pp. 8–9, 19, 23; © Archivo Iconografico, S.A./CORBIS, pp. 14–15; Courtesy Museum of the Alphabet, p. 16; © The Art Archive/University Library Coimbra/Dagli Orti, p. 20; © The Jewish Museum, NY / Art Resource, NY, p. 24; © Charles & Josette Lenars/CORBIS, p. 25; © Zev Radovan/Land of the Bible Photo Archive, Jerusalem, pp. 26, 28, 30, 30–31 (scythe), 32, 33, 37, 39, 41, 47 (all), 48, 50 (bottom), 51, 52, 53, 55 (both), 56–57, 59, 61, 62, 64, 68, 72–73, 74–75; © Eric and David Hosking/CORBIS, p. 27; © Steve Kaufman/CORBIS, p. 29; © Erich Lessing/Art Resource, NY, pp. 31 (bottom), 50 (right); © The Art Archive/Archaeological Museum Aleppo Syria/Dagli Orti, p. 34; © The Art Archive/Museo Naval Madrid/Dagli Orti, p. 35; © Hanan Isachar/CORBIS, p. 36; © Richard T. Nowitz/CORBIS, pp. 40, 42–43, 50 (top); © Jacqui Hurst/CORBIS, p. 44; © The Art Archive/Musée du Louvre Paris/Dagli Orti, p. 45; © Skirball Museum, p. 46; © The Art Archive/Dagli Orti, p. 58; © Todd Strand/Independent Picture Service, pp. 60, 66; © Raymond Gehman/CORBIS, p. 63; © The Art Archive/National Museum Karachi/Dagli Orti, p. 65; © The Art Archive/Municipal Library Mantua/Dagli Orti, p. 70 (top); © Art Resource, NY, p. 71 (bottom); © Bettmann/CORBIS, p. 71 (top).

Illustrations by Tim Parlin
Front cover: © Erich Lessing/Art Resource, NY (both).